Vala Hafstad

# NEWS MUSE

Humorous Poems
Inspired by Strange News

To my parents-in-law,
Pall and Thora,
for their encouragement.

# TABLE OF CONTENTS

## A FAIRY TALE

There once was a powerful lord.
There's nothing he couldn't afford.
His daughter was fair as can be;
On that every man did agree.

The suitors lined up at their gate.
For hours, they'd patiently wait,
But Beauty would all of them shun
And say, "Of those men I'll have none."

The father came up with a plan
And said, "I will promise the man
Who woos and wins over my girl
A treasure befitting an earl.

He need not be wealthy or smart,
Or skillful in music or art.
He may not be handsome or tall—
Just someone for whom she will fall.

I'll offer him diamonds and gold
I've earned from the stocks I have sold.
My daughter deserves a good man.
To help her, I'll do what I can."

The daughter said, "Give me a break.
I can't lead a life that is fake.
There won't be a man in my life.
I'm leaving and so is my wife."

And that is the end of the tale.
The daughter, no doubt, did prevail.
Her father let out a big sigh:
"I guess there are things you can't buy."

**BBC NEWS**: "**Hong Kong Tycoon Recruits Husband for Lesbian Daughter.**"
*26 September 2012*

"A well-known Hong Kong billionaire has offered $65m (£40m) to any man able to woo
and marry his lesbian daughter.
Property and shipping tycoon Cecil Chao publicly promised the 'marriage bounty' after
reports emerged that his daughter had wed her long-term girlfriend."

## APP TRAP

A study in Iceland has shown
That dating depends on your phone.
Avoid an incestuous trap
By using this ancestry app.

Your cousin is cute as can be,
But close on the family tree.
Don't kiss her or catch with your charm—
The app will just sound an alarm.

My friend, please be careful and wise
And follow my honest advice:
Don't count on the phone for alarm
Whenever you walk arm in arm.

The battery might be too low,
The Internet down or too slow,
Your phone may have dropped on the floor
Or taken a hit from the door.

I have a solution for you.
(It may sound a bit déjà vu.)
Just ask her her grandmother's name
And check that yours isn't the same.

**BBC WORLD SERVICE: "Icelandic Genealogy App."**
*24 April 2013*

"It has been marketed as an app that will let people in Iceland know how closely they are related, and an app that will help to prevent incest."

## THE SELECTION

We look at them all, one by one.
It gives us such pleasure and fun.
We're women who know what we need,
And now it is time to proceed.

He's colorful, humorous, smart,
And seems to appreciate art,
So strikingly handsome and strong,
But what do you think of the thong?

The next one is sensitive, frail,
Amazingly skinny and pale;
A poet who published this year—
Romantic, without a career.

Right next to him, someone well dressed,
Who seems a bit nervous and stressed.
An architect out of a job,
Who might be a bit of a snob.

And here is one holding a bat.
What could be the meaning of that?
Who knows what he's planning to hit?
I know I don't want to be it.

And this one is playing the blues.
His arms have outrageous tattoos.
He holds an expensive guitar
And looks like he might be a star.

But that one is charming as well—
Apparently went to Cornell.
His eyes are intelligent, blue.
Forgive me for liking the view.

This store, I must say, is first class.
We look at the goods through a glass.
The carts are enormous in size.
They must be: We're shopping for guys.

**BBC NEWS: "Shopping for Mr Right in Paris at the 'Adopt-a-Guy' Boutique."**
*13 September 2012*

"Shoppers hitting the streets of Paris could now be going home with a man in their shopping baskets. In the heart of one of Paris' main shopping districts, the 'adopt-a-guy' boutique opened its doors this week. It promises a shopping experience for any Parisians searching for Mr Right."

## HOT DATE

I'm writing a quick SMS.
It's faster than mail sent express.
I'm restless and sick
With love, so come quick.
My darling, I am in distress.

I'm glad I discovered this phone.
Its ratings are not overblown.
My spelling is checked
With auto-correct,
For errors it will not condone.

I do not use Facebook or tweet.
For that I am way too discreet.
I've seen people boast
Of dumb things and post
Obscenities they can't delete.

Remember the postcards of old.
I used to write words that were bold
To tell of my state.
The card might come late.
I'd panic—my love uncontrolled.

I need you, my dearest, right now.
Excuses I will not allow.
My love is complete
For now I'm in heat.
Love, Bella the beautiful cow.

**THE NEW YORK TIMES: "Swiss Cows Send Texts to Announce They're in Heat."**
*1 October 2012*

"Mr. Oesch tends a herd of dairy cattle and carries a smartphone wherever he goes.
Occasionally he gets an SMS from one of his cows."
"Mr. Oesch, 60, who cares for a herd of 44 Red Holstein and Jersey dairy cows, is helping
to test a device that implants sensors in cows to let farmers know when they are in heat."

## DENTAL PROBLEMS

The dental assistant is pretty;
Her figure is perfect; she's witty.
As if that's not enough:
In her presence it's tough
To focus on work—it's a pity.

The dentist is burning with fire.
His marital problems are dire.
The assistant must go.
If she doesn't, we know
His chances of cheating are higher.

The dental assistant was fired
Although she was widely admired.
All her work was first class,
But her boss was an ass
Who feared what he truly desired.

**THE TELEGRAPH: "Dentist Legally Allowed to Sack 'Irresistible' Assistant."**
*22 December 2012*

"A dentist acted legally when he sacked his attractive assistant because he and his wife thought the woman was a threat to their marriage, the all-male Iowa State Supreme Court ruled.
The court rule[d] unanimously that bosses can sack employees they see as an 'irresistible attraction,' even if the employees have not engaged in flirtatious behaviour or otherwise done anything wrong."

## DIWINE

My Father in Heaven,
It's almost eleven.
I sit at the bar
And smoke a cigar.

My minister told me
He'd no longer scold me
For being an ass
And skipping the mass.

He said, "Let us rather
In harmony gather,
Surrounded by cheer;
I'll buy you a beer."

And as we unwind here,
We'll certainly find here
The presence of God.
(I know it sounds odd.)

My minister knows me.
He eagerly shows me
A bottle of wine
Makes life look divine.

I start to hear voices.
He offers me choices:
There's whiskey and gin;
It isn't a sin.

For now I'm in Heaven.
It's half past eleven.
I'd never afford
Such liquor, my Lord.

But you are my Savior.
I'll change my behavior
And never miss mass
That's held 'round a glass.

**NPR: "To Stave Off Decline, Churches Attract New Members With Beer."**
*3 November 2013*

"With mainline religious congregations dwindling across America, a scattering of churches is trying to attract new members by creating a different sort of Christian community. They are gathering around craft beer.
Some church groups are brewing it themselves, while others are bring[ing] the Holy Mysteries to a taproom."

## TIED UP

Don't feel too tied up to travel,
Don't feel too tied up to fly,
Avoid being glued to your gadgets—
With us you can sail through the sky.

Imagine yourself on our aircraft,
Imagine yourself drinking wine.
With us you'll enjoy every moment;
The service, we promise, is fine

Unless you decide to start screaming
On board, please don't threaten or spit.
Avoid being rude or rambunctious
And don't ever grab, choke or hit,

For if you behave like a bastard,
We'll dig out our duct tape and tie,
And you'll be too tied up to struggle,
But never too tied up to fly.

**NEW YORK MAGAZINE:** "Incident Involving Drunk Icelandair Passenger Proves That Duct Tape Really Can Fix Anything."
*5 January 2013*

"Things got weird aboard a JFK-bound Icelandair flight on Thursday, when a passenger had to be tied up with duct tape and zip ties after having more than a bit too much to drink."

16

## THE MAGIC OF MIRRORS

Witness the health revolution:
Visit our grocery store.
We have the perfect solution;
This is the place to explore.

Step on a scale as you enter,
Notice your weight on a screen
Located right in the center,
Back where the clients convene.

Please take a cart for your shopping.
It has a mirror within.
Trust us, it will have a whopping
Impact on making you thin.

Then you must look at your tummy.
It will reflect in the cart.
Surely, you aren't a dummy:
Watching your front makes you smart.

You will decide to go swimming,
Jogging, or biking, at last,
Totally focused on trimming
Fat off your waist in a blast.

That's when you'll lose all your cravings,
Promise yourself to be wise,
Realize sizable savings
Skipping all burgers and fries.

Right at this moment we'll tell you
There is no food in our store,
What we are ready to sell you
Happens to matter much more.

Then you will exit elated,
Even though nothing was bought.
This is the place, long awaited,
Where we sell food just for thought.


**THE NEW YORK TIMES:** "Nudged to the Produce Aisle by a Look in the Mirror."
*27 August 2013*

"The mirror is part of an effort to get Americans to change their eating habits, by two social scientists outmaneuvering the processed-food giants on their own turf, using their own tricks: the distracting little nudges and cues that confront a supermarket shopper at every turn."

## HOSPITALITY

I'll give you a cup of coffee,
Along with a piece of toffee.
It's great to have such a guest;
You only deserve the best.

This coffee is quite expensive.
Its process is so extensive.
The beans pass a certain tract
And do not come out intact.

Their colorful shell is broken.
(Of this, many chefs have spoken.)
The bitterness goes away
With enzymes, or so they say.

The beans in which I've invested
Are known to have been digested
By animals way out east
In Asia: the civet beast.

Its excrements are collected.
Inside them, the beans detected.
They're roasted a little bit.
That's how you get gold from shit.

I thought you would be delighted.
You don't look at all excited.
I'll give you another cup...
My goodness, you're throwing up!

**YAHOO NEWS:** "The Most Expensive Coffee in the World Comes From Civet Poo, but That's Not the Bad News."
*22 April 2013*

"The civet, a small Asian mammal that looks like a cross between a weasel and a raccoon, is not just a cute logo for the brand. Civet coffee is made from coffee beans found in civet excrement. The civet's digestive enzymes ferment the beans, and after much rinsing, the beans extracted from the feces are said to make a dark, smooth, rich, smoky cup of Joe—or as one tasteless term goes, 'crappuccino.'"

## A STAR IN THE SKY

It's time for a new destination.
Just fill out a short application.
The prize is a trip to the stars.
You'll land, if you're chosen, on Mars.

No need for your rose-colored glasses.
This planet all others surpasses
In redness, as evidence shows.
La vie over there is en rose.

You may want a book in your backpack.
And maybe a super-sized snack sack.
The trip will take 200 days,
Assuming there won't be delays.

There won't be a guy there to greet you,
Or natives or waiters to meet you,
No cocktails or food on a tray.
You won't find a pub or café.

We know you're resourceful and clever
And ready for such an endeavor.
You'll figure out how to grow food.
If not, you're most certainly screwed.

We trust you're adaptable, always.
You will not find fountains in hallways.
On Mars, there's no lake and no sea.
No problem: Recycle your pee.

The landscape is truly attractive.
The air may be radioactive,
But if you get cancer up there,
We really won't bother or care.

Instead, we will watch as you wither.
We'll follow you hither and thither
With interest, while sipping our tea.
You will be a star on TV.

Imagine the gold for our station,
The drama, the series' duration!
We'll call it "The Star in the Sky."
It runs till the day that you die.


**BBC NEWS: "Applicants Wanted for a One-Way Ticket to Mars."**
*17 April 2013*

"Want to go to Mars? Dutch organisation Mars One says it will open applications
imminently. It would be a one-way trip, and the company hopes to build a community
of settlers on the planet."

## THE CHEETAHS' RESPONSE

Our life in the zoo is a pain.
We struggle for freedom in vain.
We cheetahs committed no crime,
But, yet, we were caught in our prime

And sentenced to life in a zoo.
Since then, we've been lonesome and blue.
You gave us no trial, no deal,
No chance to protest or appeal.

Don't tell us to mate behind bars.
Captivity leaves many scars.
The urge to have offspring is none.
No fire, no passion, no fun.

You've got to let all of us loose.
A partner we'll find to seduce.
Attraction is sudden, complex.
Survival depends on wild sex.

THE NEW YORK TIMES: "Date Night at the Zoo, if Rare Species Play Along."
*4 July 2012*

"With extinctions rising and habitats being destroyed, zoos are trying to breed about 160 endangered species in captivity. But while mating in the wild seems largely primal and effortless, in captivity it can be anything but."

## A LIFE OF LUXURY

During this dreadful recession,
My blog is a welcome digression.
I write about all sorts of food
That's good for my health and my mood.

I relish both puffin and pheasant;
The taste of those two is quite pleasant.
My haddock is caught on a line
In Iceland—amazingly fine.

The pumpkin I eat is organic,
Since pesticide taste makes me panic.
My mountain spring water is great.
It comes from a spring out of state.

I often have air in my belly,
The kind that is awfully smelly.
I treat it with Fart and Away—
A candle, as sweet as soufflé.

I really adore roasted turkey,
And sometimes I munch on beef jerky.
I truly love freshwater trout.
That's something I can't live without.

Organic and fair-trade quinoa
I welcome with smiles and "Aloha."
I'm crazy for meatballs with jam
And choose only nitrate-free ham.

I'm neutered, but to my amazement
I'm blessed with equipment replacement:
Prosthetic and custom-made nuts
That boost both my ego and guts.

The nuts didn't come all that cheaply.
I'm grateful for them, really deeply.
They're one thousand dollars a pair.
(My boss is a big millionaire.)

And yak's milk I drink on occasion.
It gives me a splendid sensation.
I also like butternut squash.
You see that my diet is posh.

I tell you, it's good to eat healthy.
To do so, befriend someone wealthy.
Now, thank you for reading my blog.
(In case you don't know, I'm a dog.)

**THE NEW YORK TIMES:** "' For the Dogs' Has a Whole New Meaning."
*4 June 2011*

"Pan-seared duck with brown rice and blueberry compote.
Roasted turkey with butternut squash and russet potatoes.
Salmon with black-and-white quinoa.
Delish. Just keep in mind that all of this, right down to those banana and yogurt health
bars, is dog food."
"[L]ast year, Americans spent a record $55 billion on their pets."

## MEAT TO DIE FOR

I listen to Satie,
And sometimes Debussy.
I'm treated when I dine
To beer that's very fine.
They rub my rump and loin,
My flank, and even groin.
I eat till I am full.
I am a Kobe bull.

They killed me.  Now I'm dead.
The farmer must be fed.
They say a slice of me
Is quite a luxury.
The price is in a book
Of records—take a look.

They gulp me down with wine
Or beer that's very fine,
And listen to Satie,
Or even Debussy.
They eat till they are full
Of me, the Kobe bull.

They get a belly rub
While soaking in a tub.
Some day they, too, will die.
I have to wonder why
They cannot sell their meat.
It should be quite a treat.


**NPR: "Fake Food: That's Not Kobe Beef You're Eating."**
*22 April 2012*

**WORLD ENGLISH DICTIONARY:**
"Kobe beef
Also called: Wagyu  a grade of beef from cattle raised in Kobe, Japan, which is extremely
tender and full-flavoured as a result of the cattle being massaged with sake and fed a
special diet including large quantities of beer."

## AUTO-BREWERY

I get wasted without drinking wine.
It's enough that I munch or I dine
To get totally smashed.
I am truly abashed
When I fail to walk down a straight line.

I will call it my personal ale.
It is brewed on the tiniest scale:
Not enough for a cask,
For a bottle or flask.
It is possibly dark, maybe pale.

It is made both with barley and wheat,
But the recipe isn't concrete.
I use bagels and rice,
Even pasta and pies—
Any starch that I happen to eat.

No one works in my brewery, but
Don't imagine its doors have been shut,
For I'm constantly drunk,
Simply drunk as a skunk,
With a brewery built in my gut.

NPR: "Auto-Brewery Syndrome: Apparently, You Can Make Beer in Your Gut."
*17 September 2013*

"A 61-year-old man — with a history of home-brewing — stumbled into a Texas emergency room complaining of dizziness. Nurses ran a Breathalyzer test. And sure enough, the man's blood alcohol concentration was a whopping 0.37 percent, or almost five times the legal limit for driving in Texas.
There was just one hitch: The man said that he hadn't touched a drop of alcohol that day."
"The patient had an infection with Saccharomyces cerevisiae, Cordell says. So when he ate or drank a bunch of starch — a bagel, pasta or even a soda — the yeast fermented the sugars into ethanol, and he would get drunk. Essentially, he was brewing beer in his own gut."

## MODERN MENU

The menu tonight is ambitious.
We promise it's super-delicious.
It's healthy, high protein, low fat.
We know you'll be happy with that.

It tastes very nutty and meaty
With spices from Greece and Tahiti.
Don't worry—our prices ain't steep.
This food is incredibly cheap.

We find the ingredients quickly.
Alive, they are slimy or prickly.
Some sting, others crawl, even bite,
But fried, you will love them all right.

So, don't say you're bugged by the menu.
You've entered the pestival venue.
We know there's a fly in your soup.
In fact, you just ate a whole scoop.

**BBC NEWS: "Insects Source of Protein Instead of Meat."**
*6 May 2013*

"But as the global population continues to grow, there is a growing move towards eating insects as a staple part of our diet."

## MANNERS CAFÉ

You've entered the Manners Café.
In here, you must watch what you say.
The price of our coffee is right,
As long as you're nice and polite.

We will no abruptness endure.
You've got to say "Hi" or "Bonjour."
The price of the food will increase
In case you forget to say "Please."

We trust you are fully aware
That here, it's expensive to swear,
And don't say your coffee is cold,
Your sandwiches rotten or old.

And don't say we suck or we stink,
For we do not care what you think.
Instead, you'll be punished—you will:
Your insults add up on the bill.

The truth is our coffee is cold,
Our sandwiches rotten and old.
Although this is no Cordon blue,
We don't want to hear it from you.

**THE GUARDIAN:** "French Café Offers Discounts to Polite Customers."
*11 December 2013*

"In an attempt to turn the tables on customers who complain that serving staff are rude,
the manager warned he would hit impolite customers where it hurts, in the pocket.
A sign outside the establishment states:
'Un café- €7 [£5.90]
Un café s'il vous plaît - €4.25
Bonjour, un café, s'il vous plaît - €1.40.'"

## DIAMONDS TO DIE FOR

You don't have to bury your mother,
Your father, or sister, or brother,
Your rabbit, your dog, or your cat.
Our option is better than that.

Avoid any funeral clashes;
Just send us your family's ashes.
Enclose them with ten thousand bucks.
(This service is truly deluxe.)

To ship the whole heap is expensive;
No need, though, to be apprehensive:
A pound of the person will do
To finish the process for you.

The ashes we then set afire.
(Compression is what they require.)
Voilà—and a diamond is born.
It's ready to shine and adorn.

And now you can wear it to meetings,
Or parties—imagine the greetings:
They'll ask you, "What's that on your chest?"
You'll answer, "That's Mom laid to rest."

Now, resting in peace is old-fashioned.
(Our boss, on this point, feels impassioned.)
The piece you rest in ought to shine.
In death, you'll be top-of-the-line.

**NPR: "From Ashes to Ashes to Diamonds: A Way to Treasure the Dead."**
*19 January 2014*

"Diamonds are supposed to be a girl's best friend. Now, they might also be her mother, father or grandmother.
Swiss company Algordanza takes cremated human remains and — under high heat and pressure that mimic conditions deep within the Earth — compresses them into diamonds."

# THE DOGS' WEDDING VOWS

He:
You've turned on my ecstasy switch.
I feel so incredibly rich
To call you my wife
The rest of my life.
I love you, my darling, my bitch.

She:
To you, I'm eternally bound.
What bliss, such a match to have found.
I love how you kiss
And lick up my piss,
My fearless and beautiful hound.

**BBC NEWS: "Sri Lanka Police Dog 'Weddings' Condemned by Minister."**
*28 August 2013*

"Sri Lanka's culture ministry has strongly condemned a mass 'wedding' of police dogs which they say offensively used traditional Buddhist symbols.
Police 'married' nine pairs of dogs on a platform decorated with white cloth and flowers in a ceremony resembling a traditional marriage.
The 'brides' wore mittens, shawls and hats while the 'grooms' wore red ties.
Police have defended the 'wedding' saying that it was done to promote the domestic breeding of sniffer dogs."

## CAT-ASTROPHE

A tourist must plan for a trip
To Iceland, by air or by ship.
A four-legged female needs lots
Of papers and plenty of shots.

A beauty queen came to our land,
Her trip neither thought out nor planned.
The name of this female was Nook.
She had an astonishing look.

The cat came to town in a jet,
Without getting shots from the vet.
Alone from the airport she strayed
And quarantine tried to evade.

The beauty queen, furry and black,
Was gone and might never be back.
A rescue team looked high and low.
Their worries continued to grow.

The nation enjoyed the suspense;
Its interest in Nook was immense.
With flashlights they searched by the score
And traced all the tracks by the shore.

The owner, at last, heard a meow.
She happily answered with "Ciao!"
The cat came from under a house
In which she had captured a mouse.

Authorities often are cruel,
Intent on obeying a rule.
Refusing to turn a blind eye,
They said the illegal must die.

She might have brought germs to the land
Where cats from a jet remain banned
Unless they have papers that state
Their health is determined first rate.

The tourism lobby is strong.
They saw that the measures were wrong.
To execute tourists on jets,
To them, is as bad as it gets.

They lobbied for hours on end,
Discussing the tourism trend.
To kill off a cat is a mess
And wouldn't look good in the press.

Their lobbying did save a life,
For Nookie eluded the knife.
The tourism industry thrives
And stresses it's there to save lives.

**NEWS OF ICELAND: "Danish Cat Lost in Iceland."**
*25 September 2013*

"Icelandic Food and Veterinary Authority (MAST) is afraid that Nuk might carry infectious diseases and wants the cat to be caught as soon as possible. Animals are not allowed to enter Iceland until they've been in quarantine for a while, due to the risk of rabies or other infection."

## MANSION

Our friends, in a housing expansion,
Constructed the mightiest mansion,
The largest one I've ever seen,
The rooms were at least seventeen.

They moved in and all appeared dandy.
They entertained, serving us brandy,
But, somehow, they ceased to be close.
The space was too big...well, who knows?

The husband became very distant.
The wife wished she had an assistant.
And, finally, hubbie moved out.
(The neighbors heard both of them shout.)

The lesson I've learned is that houses
Can ruin the passion of spouses,
So, homebuyers, please be aware:
Some houses are too big to share.

**MSN NEWS: "At Annual Builders' Show, Small is In."**
*2009*

## STRESS RELIEF

It's time for you all to acknowledge
That stress is a problem in college,
And stress takes a terrible toll.
We must get it under control.

In fact, we are truly delighted
To tell you we're ready to fight it:
Today we present to the press
The experts who work against stress.

Available at any hour,
An expert will use all his power
To listen and soothe every mind.
This treatment is one of a kind.

A secret he keeps without trouble:
The seal on his lips remains double.
He may not give any advice—
His presence is sure to suffice.

He may not have much education.
His language will need no translation.
His background is humble indeed;
He's never been taught how to read.

You may take him home if you're lonely.
I promise you, he is the only
Professional you can check out.
It's helpful, without any doubt.

With him at your side you'll be happy.
Your life will no longer seem crappy.
Stay close to him just for a while.
His calmness will bring you a smile.

Our experts have duties so many,
But don't earn as much as a penny.
They do not have emails or blogs.
They're certified therapy dogs.


THE WASHINGTON POST: "Cuddly Puppies Help Law Students De-Stress Before Exams."
2 December 2011

## THE ESCAPE

I escaped in the dark of the night—
Couldn't bear any longer the plight
Of my group. We were born behind bars.
Such a life leaves emotional scars.

Someone whispered the words in my ear
(To this date, who it was isn't clear).
"There's an ocean out there you must see.
Let your goal be from this to break free."

I grew stronger and stronger with time,
Strong enough to be able to climb
Up the wall, past the wire and fence.
My resolve made my vigor immense.

What a world I discovered beyond!
Until then, I had seen but a pond.
Now a river with plenty of food
Caught my eye—soon my strength was renewed.

Since that night, I have treasured each day
And enjoyed catching fish in the bay.
The authorities can't capture me.
I'm a fast-swimming, small escapee.

They have chased me by land and by sea,
And detectives have run after me.
I have managed to trace back my roots
To the land of quinoa and fruits.

All across the Pacific I'll steer.
There's no wave, not a shark that I fear.
I have relatives down in Peru.
They'll be glad I escaped from the zoo.

There will be such a feast when I land.
They will call my escape simply grand.
Then the praise of their penguin they'll sing,
Whom they're sure to take under their wing.

**BBC NEWS**: "Tokyo Search for Young Penguin Escapee."
*5 March 2012*

## IN THE ZOO

Look, here to our right is the human,
A beast most aggressive and weird.
The male is called "man," female "woman."
They once were respected and feared.

They built all the towns and the cities,
With factories, houses and schools.
They sat on a bunch of committees
And worked with a number of tools.

They often showed signs of aggression
And constantly seemed to wage war.
They suffered from plague and depression,
From ignorance, greed and much more.

They treated the planet quite badly:
Polluted the earth and the sky,
Ignored all the evidence, sadly,
And kissed preservation good-bye.

And that's when we monkeys decided
That surely enough was enough.
Those humans had been so misguided.
Now we must rebel and be tough.

We started with organized mugging,
And biting, and chasing them all,
By stealing, and teasing, and bugging.
The beast felt its confidence fall.

It didn't take long to defeat it.
The creature fled into its house.
Our regiment utterly beat it.
The beast was entrapped as a mouse.

Then most of the humans expired.
They died from pollution and flu.
Our government only required
We keep a few score in the zoo.

They serve as a sorry reminder
Of fools, who so horribly failed.
How fortunate that a much kinder,
Responsible creature prevailed.


**THE NEW YORK TIMES:** "Indians Feed the Monkeys, Which Bite the Hand."
*22 May 2012*

"Stories abound in Delhi of monkeys' entering homes, ripping out wiring, stealing clothes
and biting those who surprise them. They treat the Indian Parliament building as a
playground, have invaded the prime minister's office and Defense Ministry, sometimes
ride buses and subway trains, and chase diplomats from their well-tended gardens.
Roopi Saran, a Delhi resident, has seen monkeys steal candy from the hands of her
children. And tribes of monkeys often take over her yard, preventing her and her
children from venturing outside.
'So we sit inside our house like caged animals, like we're the ones in the zoo and they're
the owners outside looking at us,' Ms. Saran said."

## SAVING LAZY

My illness began in November,
And then, on the third of December,
They told us the tumor was bad.
My master was terribly sad.

No reason for me to be emo.
They gave me the option of chemo.
A bone-marrow transplant, they said,
Would follow, or else I'd be dead.

"It doesn't come cheap, saving Lazy.
The figures may sound kind of crazy.
My best guess is 25 grand.
Be ready next week, cash in hand."

"The kids can forget about college.
The price is too high for that knowledge.
What matters is saving her life,"
Said master, and so did his wife.

My owners collected their money.
With tears in their eyes, they said, "Honey,
Why should we accumulate wealth?
The focus should be on your health."

I noticed the children were bitter.
They said so on Facebook and Twitter.
My sickness did not make them weep.
They said euthanasia was cheap.

The hospital stay went by quickly.
For days after that I looked sickly,
But then I began to feel fine.
My owners were both on cloud nine.

But sunshine is followed by showers,
And this time the luck wasn't ours.
One day, at a quarter to three,
It struck me that I couldn't pee.

A tumor obstructed my urine,
According to Dr. Banduren.
To cure it cost many a buck
(Six thousand).  The dad sold his truck.

He had to find new transportation,
And quickly, without reservation,
Got used to the train ride to work.
(He worked at a bank as a clerk.)

Then, after they cured my last ailment,
There happened this tragic derailment.
The kids tried to blame it on me.
The widow, she seemed to agree.

The house was bereft of contentment.
I noticed an air of resentment
The next time we went to the vet.
It turned out that they were in debt.

I died about seven months later.
Their daughter, the animal-hater,
Engraved on my tombstone:  "A Bitch—
The Reason We Never Got Rich."


**THE NEW YORK TIMES:** "New Treatments to Save a Pet, but Questions About the Costs."
*5 April 2012*

## NEW FLU

Be aware of the new kind of flu.
There is nothing at all you can do
To avoid getting sick—
Washing hands ain't the trick;
There's no shot, no prevention for you.

If you catch it, your dad is to blame,
Or your mother, their wealth, or their fame.
They said, "Don't be afraid;
We will come to your aid;
It's all right if you kill or you maim."

They have taught you what money can buy:
There's no limit to that but the sky.
Be it access or A's,
Even justice, these days,
Is for sale when your status is high.

There's a new kind of flu that we fear;
It is not influenza that's here,
But our worries have grown,
For our research has shown
Affluenza is much more severe.

**BBC NEWS: "'Affluenza Defence': Rich, Privileged and Unaccountable."**
*13 December 2013*

"Is there a separate justice system in the US for the rich and powerful? It all depends on whether you believe that Ethan Couch would be in jail right now were it not for his wealthy parents and privileged background.

On 15 June, Ethan, 16, was driving with a blood-alcohol level three times above the legal limit. He lost control of his speeding pick-up truck and killed four pedestrians. On Tuesday, he was sentenced to serve in a high-priced California drug rehabilitation centre paid for by the parents, with no jail time and 10 years of probation.

It's the court case that has made the 'affluenza defence' a household word, as Ethan's lawyers successfully argued he had a diminished sense of responsibility due to his wealth, pampered childhood, and absentee parenting."

# A PRAYER

My Father, thou who art up there,
I hope you hear my humble prayer.
My congregation is upset;
They say I've got to pay my debt.

I want my Heaven here on Earth;
That's why I've served you since my birth.
I've built myself a fancy home
That doesn't please the guy in Rome.

But think about it, dearest Dad,
There's reason for you to be glad,
For every good and loyal son
Undoubtedly deserves some fun.

I've sacrificed so much for you:
A woman I may not pursue.
Since I may never have a spouse,
My compensation is this house.

So, let me keep my gilded doors,
My jewels and my chest of drawers,
My sauna, bathtub and my wine,
The table where I sit and dine.

I know they're not the cheapest kind;
My taste is said to be refined.
IKEA simply ain't my thing,
Your son, the bishop, nicknamed Bling.

**BBC NEWS: "Vatican Suspends 'Bishop of Bling' Tebartz-van Elst."**
*23 October 2013*

"The Vatican has suspended a senior German Church leader dubbed the 'bishop of bling' by the media over his alleged lavish spending.
Bishop of Limburg Franz-Peter Tebartz-van Elst is accused of spending more than 31m euros (£26m; $42m) on renovating his official residence."

## SWAN SONG

The trial is beginning;
I'm ready in defense.
The outlook is alarming;
I'm feeling rather tense.
I know I killed a person
Who trespassed to my land.
This didn't have to happen,
But things got out of hand.
I do admit I'm sorry,
Although I had the right
To guard against invaders
Who threaten, day and night.
The victim ruffled feathers,
And I became upset.
His presence seemed to tell me
He posed a real threat.
No wonder I am shaking;
I am a nervous wreck,
For if they find me guilty,
They'll hang me by the neck.
It's early in the morning.
The judge conceals a yawn,
"Please state your name," he's roaring.
I answer, "It is Swan."

**NEW YORK DAILY NEWS:** "Illinois Man Drowns in Pond After Freak Encounter
With Swans."
*16 April 2012*

## AT THE GALLERY

The theme in this painting is Norse.
It's clear that it's painted with force.
Who makes such art?
Let's check the chart...
Apparently, it is a horse.

The next work is titled "A Gnat."
Spectacular job, notice that.
In every line
The work is fine.
The artist, I'm told, is a cat.

Here's one that is titled "A Log."
With plenty of darkness and fog.
It's mostly gray,
But, anyway,
Quite good for a ten-year-old dog.

The work that we're looking at now
Reminds me of pasture, somehow.
It's very green
And quite pristine.
No wonder...it's made by a cow.

The rumors you're hearing are true.
The arts are becoming a zoo.
Without a paw
Or hoof or claw,
No fame or exhibit for you.

DIE WELT: "Horse Chosen to Exhibit Artwork in Italy."
*17 October 2008*

## EYE-PHONE

The iPhone 5 in pink or blue
Is what we want to sell to you.
We know the iPhone is a must.
If you can't buy it, bite the dust.

We offer you a special deal.
This offer has a wide appeal.
You will not need a card or cash.
Our business model is a smash.

It's bartering that saves your day.
We know you have the means to pay,
So even if you're broke or blue,
Let's make this happen, just for you.

We'll take your baby if she's cute.
Just drop her in the baby chute.
Your in-laws we can take as well,
Although they will be hard to sell.

A slice of liver might just do.
The case will cost a toe or two.
We'll take your kidney, arm or eye.
You'll do without them, by and by.

And if your socket ever aches,
A painkiller is all it takes.
You'll leave our store a lucky guy.
We are the Apple of your eye.

**THE SYDNEY MORNING HERALD:** "Couple in China 'Sell' Baby Daughter for iPhone."
*21 October 2013*

**DIGITAL JOURNAL:** "Chinese Teen Sells Kidney for iPad and iPhone."
*7 April 2012*

## DARK ADVICE

No reason to go to the gym
Or diet to stay very slim,
But what you must do
Is easy for you:
The lights in the house you must dim.

The experts say people eat less
When lighting is not in excess.
Just turn off the light
Completely tonight.
Your weight you will quickly address.

In darkness you can't overeat.
A diet like this you can't beat:
You won't find your fork,
Potato or pork,
Your pudding, your pickle or meat.

You hibernate—that is the thing!
Imagine what darkness can bring.
Just act like a bear,
Curl up in your lair
And wake up quite slim in the spring.

## A READER'S RESPONSE

My chances of slimming are slight.
I don't have a dimmable light,
But what's even worse
(It's some kind of curse):
My vision is perfect at night.

CORNELL UNIVERSITY FOOD AND BRAND LAB: "Lighting and Music Affect Food Consumption and Satisfaction in Surprising Ways."
2012

# PERSONAL AD

An ugly, unusual male,
Whose life has been spent in a jail,
Seeks female as ugly as him.
(His chances, he reckons, are slim.)

His record will surely appall:
A female he killed in a brawl.
Remorseless, he shouted with glee,
"There's plenty of fish in the sea."

But now he is ugly and old
And knows he will not be paroled.
A female he needs to ensure
His species will safely endure.

And this is his desperate plea.
He needs someone a.s.a.p.
His ad and his future are linked:
Without a reply, he's extinct.

The male is a tropical fish,
A cichlid, whose ultimate wish
Is finding a female before
His type won't exist anymore.

So, males, learn a lesson from him,
Whose chances are terribly slim:
The fish in the sea may be few,
Created precisely for you.

**BBC NEWS: "Zoo Seeks Mate for Last Surviving 'Gorgeously Ugly' Fish."**
*10 May 2013*

"The Zoo, which describes the fish as 'gorgeously ugly', is hoping to start a conservation programme if a fit female can be found for the captive males.
And with two of the males now 12 years old, the quest is said to be extremely urgent."
"There are two males in captivity at London Zoo and another in Berlin. There had been a female in captivity at the German zoo but attempts to breed ended in disaster when the male killed her."

## LOST AND FOUND

We search for so much in our lives:
For love and for husbands and wives,
For meaning, compassion and hope,
Or someone with whom to elope.

We look for a room with a view,
For passions we want to pursue,
For diets that do not depress,
Or jobs without worry or stress.

And often our mind will not rest,
For we can be truly distressed
If we cannot find what is lost—
A search for oneself can exhaust.

This happened to someone I know:
To Iceland, alone, did she go.
She walked off her bus dressed in black,
But wore something red coming back.

In red, no one knew who she was.
Apparently, it was because
In red, she looked young and so fair.
Besides, she had tied back her hair.

But where was the woman in black?
She left and she never came back.
They searched by the canyon and stream.
My friend, dressed in red, joined the team.

She crossed over glacier and ice
And covered some areas twice.
Exhausted, she came to a creek.
The water was clear—how unique!

Her face was reflected right there
And, suddenly, she was aware
The woman she thought might have drowned,
Was she—yes, herself—she was found!

**ICELAND REVIEW: "Lost Woman Looks for Herself in Iceland's Highlands."**
*27 August 2012*

"A foreign tourist was reported missing in the volcanic canyon Eldgjá in the southern highlands on Saturday afternoon after she failed to return to her tour bus. The driver waited for about one hour before notifying the police and continuing the tour.

Search and rescue were sent to the area shortly afterwards. However, the search was called off at 3 am when it turned out that the missing woman had been on the bus all along and even participated in the search for herself, mbl.is reports.

Before reentering the bus after the stop at Eldgjá, the woman had changed her clothes and freshened up, resulting in the other passengers not recognizing her."

## WARNING SIGNS

You speed through stop signs,
Dying to show up early
For your funeral.

Time is limited.
You write your last text message.
That's when it hits you.

You are unrestrained,
Free from the choking seatbelt.
You love it to death.

Heed the speed limit
Or you'll end up really slow,
Leaning on crutches.

Jaywalking tempts you.
Halfway across it strikes you
As a big mistake.

Calling your girlfriend
On the cell phone in traffic,
You end up crushed.

Mascara applied
At a red light, then a crash.
She turns a blind eye.

Intoxicated
You bump into bystanders.
Sobering outcome.

Exhausted you drive,
Doze off for just a moment.
This is your nightmare.

A loud stereo
Blocks out the sound of sirens.
You will hear no more.

You feel really hot
When racing another car.
Your burning problem.

Donations welcome
From those who wear no helmet.
No tax deduction.

**THE NEW YORK TIMES**: "Traffic Warnings, 17 Syllables a Sign."
*29 November 2011*

## GRANDPA DIES—MAYBE

We were shocked to see grandfather croak.
What a prankster he'd been, the old bloke.
His heart did not beat.
Our grief was complete
When we figured his death was a joke.

As the hearse drove away down the hill,
He deceived us completely until
He opened his eyes,
Said, "Not so fast, guys!
I've decided to rewrite my will."

And our grandpa came back undeterred.
What he did the next day was absurd:
He fell on his head,
Said, "This time I'm dead."
Should we take the old man at his word?

**ABC NEWS: "Miss. Man, Declared Dead, Wakes up in Body Bag at Funeral Home."**
*28 February 2014*

**CBS NEWS: "Mississippi Man Who Woke up in Body Bag 2 Weeks Ago Has Died."**
*13 March 2014*

## TICKS

We are plagued by the worst kinds of ticks,
And against them there is not a fix.
If they bite you, infection comes fast
And the damage is heavy and vast.

They won't kill, but the victims will change
And begin to act distant and strange.
At the outset, the victims imply
They're compassionate—that's just a lie.

They will promise to give you a voice
And reiterate you'll have a choice,
But as long as they're plagued by this pest,
They will fail every confidence test.

As Samaritans they'll masquerade
And betray every promise they've made.
Once they've mastered deception and tricks,
There's no cure for corrupt poli-ticks.

## DISASTER DAYS

Our village deserves some attention.
It's time that we held a convention.
I think it is safe to presume
We're experts in sadness and gloom.

We need a good name for the meeting
A name that our guests like repeating.
"Disaster Days" doesn't sound bad;
The mood will be somber and sad.

Our local, ambitious committee
Arranged for a class in self-pity.
We'll cry and complain as a team.
"Our life is a mess" is the theme.

There will be a book competition.
You'll read from your latest edition.
No thought in the book may be deep.
The winner will put us to sleep.

On Saturday night we'll serve dinner.
The chef is a total beginner.
The menu will hardly impress:
Your stomach will be in distress.

But if you can stand after dinner,
You could be the ballroom dance winner.
Don't worry—we will not have pros:
You'll win just by stepping on toes.

You'll all get to practice your voices;
We'll offer you several choices
Of lessons by lovely Miss June.
She'll teach you to sing out of tune.

On Sunday, the mass will be boring.
The normal reaction is snoring.
Our priest has no humor at all.
He'll say life is hopeless for y'all.

And then you'll go home in a hurry;
You'll leave with no care and no worry.
One day you'll be back, we assume.
Our town is a dumpsite for gloom.

**ICELAND REVIEW: "Looking for Disaster? Head to Hólmavík."**
*12 February 2014*

"The festival Hörmungardagar, or Disaster Days, will be held in Hólmavík in the West Fjords' Strandir region, for the first time this weekend. This new cultural Friday to Sunday festival will have both local and foreign participants, from Finland and Canada, bb.is reports.
On Friday's program, among other activities, is a course in self-pity, a complaint service and an ugly dance performance."

## TALENT RETURNS

Our government is good and smart.
It never fails to play its part.
And now it has the perfect plan
To tempt the educated man.

The knowledgeable and the bright
Are ready now to book a flight.
They left a country lost in debt
Where unemployment posed a threat.

But clever rulers find a way
To stop the flow to USA,
To Europe, Asia—anywhere.
They've got to show they really care.

They'll bring the expats back on planes
And show them they can use their brains.
Creative minds will get a chance
To help their countrymen advance.

The talented are in demand.
They'll be rewarded in this land.
Of hopes and dreams there is no lack.
They'll all be happy to be back.

The nation's ills can now be cured.
Prosperity will be ensured.
What cures what seemed refractory?
A fertilizer factory.


**ICELAND REVIEW:** "Talent Returns."
*5 March 2014*

A recent report from Iceland's Progressive Party MPs states the party's interest in investigating the feasibility of constructing a fertilizer factory as soon as possible in the towns of Helguvík or Þorlákshöfn. The party stresses the importance of "instilling hope in the hearts of young Icelanders" and "enticing Icelandic expats back home."

## WARNING

I'm stunning, magnificent, white;
To artists, a constant delight.
My picture adorns many walls
Of dining rooms, offices, halls.

My figure is perfect; I'm swell.
I do have a temper as well:
The anger is boiling within—
An outburst about to begin.

I'm sick of the state of our land
Where hooligans are in command.
For nature they have no respect,
Refusing our parks to protect.

Beware of my temper!  Stay back!
I'm having an anger attack
And switching to fiery mode.
I'm Hekla—about to explode.

ICELAND REVIEW: "Hekla Volcano Could Erupt Soon."
*17 March 2014*

## PM ON UN CLIMATE REPORT

The UN report appears frightful;
To us, though, it's simply delightful.
We shouldn't succumb to such fear,
But focus on laughter and cheer.

The problems abroad do not matter.
To me, they are meaningless chatter.
And why should I care about drought
In lands I know nothing about?

They talk of the sea level rising.
It doesn't sound all that surprising.
So what, if the snow cover shrinks?
It isn't as bad as one thinks.

For here is our chance to make money.
The future for us appears sunny.
It's good to get rid of the ice:
A cruise on the Pole will be nice.

And just as the weather gets nicer
Up here, in the land of the Geyser,
We'll cultivate barley and wheat,
And corn that's delicious and sweet.

You know we have plenty of rivers.
I'm truly a man who delivers.
They're cash cows, as everyone knows,
So dam them is what I propose.

And damn all the press and petitions,
And critics of auto emissions.
The trees in our country ain't tall;
No reason to hug them at all.


**ICELAND REVIEW: "PM Causes Controversy over Climate Change Comments."**
*3 April 2014*

"Prime Minister of Iceland Sigmundur Davíð Gunnlaugsson said in an interview with RÚV earlier this week that although climate change has serious negative impacts for the world overall, it may create opportunities for Icelanders through food production and exports."

## ROYAL MYSTERY

An expert in royal behinds
Suspects there are criminal minds
To blame for the beautiful rear
We praised as the rear of the year.

He tells us it was but a fake:
A filling a tailor could make.
We called it "miraculous bum."
How stupid, how gullible, dumb!

The tailor created a star.
Admirers came from afar
With offers of silver and gold—
Idolatry quite uncontrolled.

The expert can offer no proof.
No reason to go through the roof.
An expert in asses of kings
Can't get to the bottom of things.

THE HUFFINGTON POST UNITED KINGDOM: "French Accuse Pippa Middleton of Wearing 'False Bottom' at Royal Wedding."
1 May 2014

Thank you for reading my book.
I hope it brightened your day. If it did, please help me spread the word by liking it on Facebook or writing a review on Amazon.com, Goodreads.com or at your favorite online store.

Best wishes,
Vala Hafstad

# BIBLIOGRAPHY

Caulfield, Philip. "Illinois man drowns in pond after freak encounter with swans." NY Daily News. N.p., 16 Apr. 2012. Web. 17 Apr. 2012.
<http://www.nydailynews.com/news/national/illinois-man-drowns-pond-freak-encounter-swans-article-1.1062266>.

"At annual builders' show, small is in - MSN Real Estate." Real Estate. N.p., n.d. Web. 26 Apr. 2014.
<http://realestate.msn.com/article.aspx?cp-documentid=17092507>.

Bankoff, Caroline . "Duct Tape Restrained Drunk Icelandair Passenger." Daily Intelligencer. N.p., 5 Jan. 2013. Web. 6 Jan. 2013.
<http://nymag.com/daily/intelligencer/2013/01/duct-tape-restrained-drunk-icelandair-passenger.html>.

Bichell, Rae. "From Ashes To Ashes To Diamonds: A Way To Treasure The Dead." NPR. NPR, 19 Jan. 2014. Web. 20 Jan. 2014.
<http://www.npr.org/2014/01/19/263128098/swiss-company-compresses-cremation-ashes-into-diamonds>.

Burnett, John. "To Stave Off Decline, Churches Attract New Members With Beer." NPR. NPR, 3 Nov. 2013. Web. 4 Nov. 2013.
<http://www.npr.org/blogs/thesalt/2013/11/03/242301642/to-stave-off-decline-churches-attract-new-members-with-beer>.

"Couple in China 'sell' baby daughter for iPhone." The Sydney Morning Herald. N.p., 21 Oct. 2013. Web. 22 Oct. 2013.
<http://www.smh.com.au/digital-life/mobiles/couple-in-china-sell-baby-daughter-for-iphone-20131021-2vwiq.html>.

"Danish Cat lost in Iceland - ISK 100.000 Reward." News of Iceland. N.p., 25 Sept. 2013. Web. 26 Sept. 2013.
<http://www.newsoficeland.com/home/culture/daily-life/item/2303-danish-cat-is-lost-in-iceland-isk-100000-reward>.

Doucleff, Michaeleen. "Auto-Brewery Syndrome: Apparently, You Can Make Beer In Your Gut." NPR. NPR, 17 Sept. 2013. Web. 18 Sept. 2013.
<http://www.npr.org/blogs/thesalt/2013/09/17/223345977/auto-brewery-syndrome-apparently-you-can-make-beer-in-your-gut>.

"Fake Food: That's Not Kobe Beef You're Eating." NPR. NPR, 22 Apr. 2012. Web. 23 Apr. 2012.
<http://www.npr.org/2012/04/22/151153503/fake-food-thats-not-kobe-beef-youre-eating>.

Grimes, William. "New Treatments to Save a Pet, but Questions About the Costs." The New York Times. The New York Times, 5 Apr. 2012. Web. 5 Apr. 2012.
<http://www.nytimes.com/2012/04/06/us/new-treatments-to-save-a-pet-but-questions-about-the-costs.html?pagewanted=all&gwh=DAE2DCA423F443D297D5B57E3FA33ABD&gwt=regi>.

Grynbaum, Michael M. "Traffic Warnings, 17 Syllables a Sign." The New York Times-City Room Blog. The New York Times, 29 Nov. 2011. Web. 29 Nov. 2011.
<http://cityroom.blogs.nytimes.com/2011/11/29/seventeen-syllable-safety-warning-signs>.

Hafstad, Vala. "Talent Returns (VH)." Iceland Review. Benedikt Jóhannesson, 5 Mar. 2014. Web. 5 Mar. 2014.
<http://icelandreview.com/stuff/views/2014/03/05/talent-returns-vh>.

Harris, Gardiner. "Indians Feed the Monkeys, Which Bite the Hand." The New York Times. The New York Times, 22 May 2012. Web. 23 May 2012.
<http://www.nytimes.com/2012/05/23/world/asia/fed-by-indians-monkeys-overwhelm-delhi.html>.

Hogenboom, Melissa. "Applicants wanted: One-way ticket to Mars." BBC News. BBC, 17 Apr. 2013. Web. 18 Apr. 2013.
<http://www.bbc.com/news/science-environment-22146456>.

"Hong Kong tycoon recruits husband for lesbian daughter." BBC News. BBC, 26 Sept. 2012. Web. 26 Sept. 2012. <http://www.bbc.com/news/world-asia-19733003>.

"Horse chosen to exhibit artwork in Italy." DIE WELT. N.p., 17 Oct. 2008. Web. 18 Oct. 2008.
<http://www.welt.de/english-news/article2590991/Horse-chosen-to-exhibit-artwork-in-Italy.html>.

"Icelandic Genealogy App." BBC News. BBC, 24 Apr. 2013. Web. 24 Apr. 2013.
<http://www.bbc.co.uk/programmes/p0175wbv>.

Johnson, Jenna. "Cuddly puppies help law students de-stress before exams." Washington Post. The Washington Post, 4 Dec. 2011. Web. 5 Dec. 2011.
<http://www.washingtonpost.com/local/education/cuddly-puppies-help-law-students-de-stress-before-exams/2011/12/01/gIQA0s9LIO_story.html>.

Kaufman, Leslie. "Date Night at the Zoo, if Rare Species Play Along." The New York Times. The New York Times, 4 July 2012. Web. 4 July 2012.
<http://www.nytimes.com/2012/07/05/science/matchmaking-at-zoos-is-rising-for-threatened-species.html?pagewanted=all>.

"Kobe beef." Dictionary.com. Dictionary.com, n.d. Web. 26 Apr. 2014.
<http://dictionary.reference.com/browse/kobe beef>.

"Lost Woman Looks for Herself in Iceland's Highlands." Iceland Review. Benedikt Jóhannesson, 27 Aug. 2012. Web. 28 Aug. 2012.
<http://icelandreview.com/news/2012/08/27/lost-woman-looks-herself-icelands-highlands>.

Maguire, John. "Insects source of protein instead of meat." BBC News. BBC, 6 May 2013. Web. 7 May 2013. <http://www.bbc.com/news/world-europe-22423977>.

Martin, Andrew. "'For the Dogs' Has a Whole New Meaning." The New York Times. The New York Times, 4 June 2011. Web. 4 June 2011. <http://www.nytimes.com/2011/06/05/business/05pets.html?pagewanted=all>.

McGrath, Matt. "Zoo seeks mate for last surviving 'gorgeously ugly' fish." BBC News. BBC, 10 May 2013. Web. 11 May 2013. <http://www.bbc.com/news/science-environment-22468206>.

"Mississippi man who woke up in body bag 2 weeks ago has died." CBSNews. CBS Interactive, 13 Mar. 2014. Web. 13 Mar. 2014. <http://www.cbsnews.com/news/mississippi-man-who-woke-up-in-body-bag-2-weeks-ago-has-died/>.

Moisse, Katie. "Miss. Man, Declared Dead, Wakes Up in Body Bag at Funeral Home." ABC News. ABC News Network, 28 Feb. 2014. Web. 28 Feb. 2014. <http://abcnews.go.com/blogs/health/2014/02/28/miss-man-declared-dead-wakes-up-in-body-bag/>.

Moss, Michael. "Nudged to the Produce Aisle by a Look in the Mirror." The New York Times. The New York Times, 27 Aug. 2013. Web. 28 Aug. 2013. <http://www.nytimes.com/2013/08/28/dining/wooing-us-down-the-produce-aisle.html?pagewanted=all>.

Mullins, KJ. "Chinese teen sells kidney for iPad and iPhone." Digital Journal. N.p., 7 Apr. 2012. Web. 8 Apr. 2012. <http://digitaljournal.com/article/322576>.

"Oh Derrier! Pippa Middleton Wore 'False Bottom' At Royal Wedding, Say French." The Huffington Post UK. N.p., 1 May 2014. Web. 2 May 2014. <http://www.huffingtonpost.co.uk/2014/05/01/pippa-middleton-bottom-royal-wedding-fake_n_5246866.html>.

Robert, Zoë«. "PM Causes Controversy over Climate Change Comments." Iceland Review. Benedikt Jóhannesson, 3 Apr. 2014. Web. 3 Apr. 2014. <http://icelandreview.com/news/2014/04/03/pm-causes-controversy-over-climate-change-comments>.

"Shopping for Mr Right in Paris." BBC News. BBC, 13 Sept. 2012. Web. 14 Sept. 2012. <http://www.bbc.com/news/world-19581307>.

"Sri Lanka police dog 'weddings' condemned by minister." BBC News. BBC, 28 Aug. 2013. Web. 28 Aug. 2013. <http://www.bbc.com/news/world-asia-23849354>.

Stefánsson, Páll. "Looking for Disaster? Head to Hólmavik." Iceland Review. Benedikt Jóhannesson, 12 Feb. 2014. Web. 12 Feb. 2014. <http://icelandreview.com/news/2014/02/12/looking-disaster-head-holmavik>.

Stefánsson, Páll. "Hekla Volcano 'Could Erupt Soon.'" Iceland Review. Benedikt Jóhannesson, 17 Mar. 2014. Web. 17 Mar. 2014. <http://icelandreview.com/news/2014/03/17/hekla-volcano-could-erupt-soon>.

Tagliabue, John. "Swiss Cows Send Texts to Announce They're in Heat." The New York Times. The New York Times, 1 Oct. 2012. Web. 1 Oct. 2012. <http://www.nytimes.com/2012/10/02/world/europe/device-sends-message-to-swiss-farmer-when-cow-is-in-heat.html?_r=2&>.

Telegraph Reporters. "Dentist legally allowed to sack 'irresistible' assistant." The Telegraph. Telegraph Media Group, 22 Aug. 2012. Web. 22 Aug. 2012. <http://www.telegraph.co.uk/news/worldnews/northamerica/usa/9762472/Dentist-legally-allowed-to-sack-irresistible-assistant.html>.

"The Most Expensive Coffee in the World Comes From Civet Poo, but That's Not the Bad News." Yahoo! News. Yahoo!, 22 Apr. 2013. Web. 23 Apr. 2013. <http://news.yahoo.com/most-expensive-coffee-world-comes-civet-poo-not-181740958.html>.

"Tokyo search for young penguin escapee." BBC News. BBC, 3 May 2012. Web. 3 May 2012. <http://www.bbc.co.uk/news/world-asia-17254650>.

"Vatican suspends 'bishop of bling'." BBC News. BBC, 23 Oct. 2013. Web. 23 Oct. 2013. <http://www.bbc.com/news/world-europe-24638430>.

Wansink, B., and K. Van Ittersum. "Lighting and music affect food consumption and satisfaction in surprising ways ." Cornell University Food and Brand Lab. Cornell University, n.d. Web. 26 Apr. 2014. <http://foodpsychology.cornell.edu/outreach/fastfood.html>.

Willsher, Kim. "French cafe offers discounts to polite customers." theguardian.com. Guardian News and Media, 12 Dec. 2013. Web. 12 Dec. 2013. <http://www.theguardian.com/world/2013/dec/11/french-cafe-discounts-police-customers>.

Zurcher, Anthony . "'Affluenza defence': Rich, privileged and unaccountable." BBC News. BBC, 13 Dec. 2013. Web. 14 Dec. 2013. <http://www.bbc.com/news/blogs-echochambers-25374458>.

Made in the USA
Monee, IL
07 May 2022